To: T

Wishing you days filled with sweet memories! Thanks for your friendship over the years!

Have a Ball!

Love,

MW00510685

Tell Me Something
Sweet

Over 150 Chocolate Quotes

by Jerry Swain

FOUNDER OF JER'S CHOCOLATES

Published by
Have a Ball
Solana Beach, California
2014

First Edition

ISBN 978-0-9910972-0-3

Tell Me Something Sweet: Over 150 Chocolate Quotes is published by:
Have A Ball Publishing Company
Solana Beach, California 92075

For information please direct emails to:
info@jerryswain.com or visit our website:
www.jerryswain.com

Edited by: Eva Shaw
Cover design, book layout and typography: Teri Rider
Photo credit, pages 29, 41, 93, 119, 134: Koelnmesse

Printed in the United States of America

00 19 18 17 16 15 14   1 2 3 4 5 6 7 8 9

Dedication

With all my love for my children, Jason and Sophia, with whom I have received such tremendous fulfillment watching as they grew from babies to toddlers to incredible small people with their own identities. Their sweet sayings have been an inspiration in compiling the sweet quotes listed in this book.

Acknowledgement

A giant thank you to all of my friends and colleagues who have supported me, my family and our chocolate business. And to our customers because without you we'd have no business and I'd probably still be figuring out my passion while eating a bowl of ice cream. Not a day goes by when I don't think about the support system I have and how lucky and fortunate I am for it.

To my parents, John and Lucy, who encouraged me to take risks, seek my passion and led by example about how to treat your friends and neighbors.

Thanks to the creative and dedicated team who spearheaded the compilation of this book including Eva Shaw, Terri Marshall and Teri Rider.

To my wife, Mariella, who has supported me and centered me in this crazy journey from an IBM-er through my idea of starting my own business. Her devotion, gentleness and support continue to provide inspiration every single day. None of this would have been possible without her.

My hope is that you enjoy this compilation of chocolate-related quotes, pick out your favorites and share them with friends. Create happiness, enjoy your journey and *Have a Ball!*

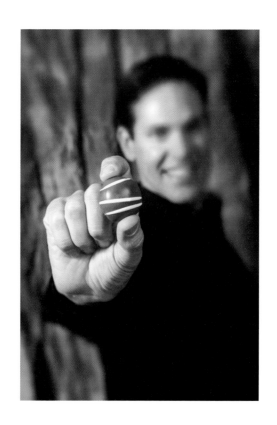

Having a Ball
Jer's Story

If the only contribution Jerry Swain ever made to this world was the decision to become a chocolatier and start Jer's Chocolates — well, that would have certainly made the world a sweeter place to live. But Jerry Swain doesn't just contribute chocolate. His contributions reach out to the community, touch lives, inspire young people and generally just make this world a bit more delicious.

Taking a break from December exams while attending the University of California, Riverside, Jerry Swain, aka "Jer," took his favorite foods and created unique peanut butter balls smothered in rich chocolate and brought them to his friends in the dormitory. The wildly popular confections were affectionately called "Jer's Balls" by his college friends. At holiday time each year, they became so much in demand that Jer enlisted friends to help create batch after delicious batch. During his years in the high-tech industry, Jer hosted an annual holiday party with one goal in mind: to bring friends together for a fun-filled evening and for a worthy cause (raising money for the food bank). Of course, Jer made the chocolate peanut butter balls. It was expected. The party became known as "Jer's Ball" by friends and created lasting memories for everyone who attended (some would say "over-the-top" fun!). That annual event continued for a decade, hosting thousands while giving back to the community with generous donations to food banks.

It was one of those balls that inspired Jer to step away from a successful high-tech career. At IBM, where he was a rising star, he earned the prestigious Rookie of the Year award and several annual performance awards. After a few more years taking on another executive position, Jer got the entrepreneurial bug and knew it was time to take on a bigger challenge. For Jer, this risk was essential in order to follow his dream and create a company built on passion, fun and philanthropy. As a result of a bit of soul searching — and with a heart-to-heart conversation and encouragement from his dad — Jer took the leap into following his dream with its core centered on chocolate and peanut butter. (Today, corporate America and universities around the country ask Jer to speak about his story, taking risks and not to fear failure.) Expressing his fun-loving side, Jer often says, "It took 'balls'" for him to make the leap. It's no wonder why "Have a Ball" has become the company tagline.

Through trial and error, hard work and lessons learned, Jer and the company continue to take enormous pride in creating premium, all-natural confections that are environmentally responsible. He has fun introducing new products and loves seeing customers take their first bite.

Although Jer has excelled at creating all-natural, award-winning chocolate delights, his philanthropic soul could never rest just with a successful chocolate business. Giving back to the community has always been part of the fabric of Jer's life. Jer is just a regular, fun-loving guy who thrives on making people happy and giving back to the community with Jer's Chocolates. A tireless volunteer for more than twenty years, Jer created Jer's Cares, the charitable initiative of the company, which is true to its roots and continues to support nonprofit organizations.

For those who know Jer personally, it will be no surprise that he's compiled a book of chocolate quotes. In every box of Jer's Chocolates, there is a quote card that is fun and/or inspirational. His compilation of quotes is his way to share a moment of fun or give you a quick laugh or smile, going along with Jer's zeal for life and love for people.

If you'd like to order more copies of this book, please visit www.jerryswain.com. For more about Jer, the inspirational Jer's Chocolates Story, or to buy products, please visit Jer's website at www.jers.com.

If you have a Jer's Chocolates story you'd like to share, please send it to Jer at Chocolate Stories, c/o Jer's Chocolates, P.O. Box 801, Solana Beach, CA 92075

THE

Chocolate

Quotes

"Chocolate is cheaper than therapy, and you don't need an appointment."

— Jill Shalvis, *Lucky in Love*

"All you need is love. But a little chocolate now and then doesn't hurt."

— *Charles M. Schulz*

"You are never alone with a bar of chocolate."

— *Anonymous*

"After eating chocolate you feel godlike, as though you can conquer enemies, lead armies, entice lovers."

— Emily Luchetti

"Money talks. Chocolate sings."

— *Anonymous*

"So much chocolate; so little time."

— *Anonymous*

"I was like a chocolate in a box, looking well behaved and perfect in place, all the while harboring a secret center."

— Deb Caletti, *Honey, Baby, Sweetheart*

"A balanced diet is chocolate in both hands."

— *Anonymous*

"Your hand and your mouth agreed many years ago that, as far as chocolate is concerned, there is no need to involve your brain."

— *Dave Barry*

"A chocolate in the mouth is worth two on the plate."

— *Anonymous*

"Do not disturb: Chocolate fantasy in progress."

— *Anonymous*

"Chocolate — It flatters you for a while; it warms you for an instant; then, all of a sudden, it kindles a mortal fever in you."

— *Madame de Sevigne*

"God gave the angels wings, and he gave humans chocolate."

— *Anonymous*

"The superiority of chocolate,
both for health and nourishment,
will soon give it the same
preference over tea and coffee in
America which it has in Spain."

— *Thomas Jefferson*

"Chocolate doesn't ask
silly questions. Chocolate
understands."

— *Anonymous*

"Every girl should have a
rendezvous with chocolate."

— *Anonymous*

"Caramels are only a fad.
Chocolate is a permanent thing."

— *Milton Snavely Hershey*

"Will sell husband for chocolate.
All sales final. No refunds.
No exchanges."

— *Anonymous*

"My favorite thing in the world
is a box of fine European
chocolates which is, for sure,
better than sex."

— *Alicia Silverstone*

"There is but one path to inner peace you seek: Chocolate."

— *Anonymous*

"A little chocolate is like a love affair — an occasional sweet release that lightens the spirit. A lot of chocolate is like marriage. It seems so good at first but before you know it you've got chunky hips and a waddle-walk."

— *Linda Solegato*

"There are times when chocolate really can fix all your problems."

— *Anonymous*

"If there's no chocolate in Heaven, I'm not going."

— Jane Seabrook, *Furry Logic Laugh at Life*

"Nine out of ten people like chocolate. The tenth person always lies."

—*John G Tullius*

"Stress would not be so hard to take if it was chocolate coated."

— *Anonymous*

"We should rejoice that
a chocolate dessert can
bring so much innocent
pleasure, even when a little
wickedness is insinuated."

— *Marcel Desaulniers*

"And above all. Think chocolate."

— *Betty Crocker*

"Chocolate causes certain endocrine glands to secrete hormones that affect your feelings and behavior by making you happy. Therefore, it counteracts depression, in turn reducing the stress of depression. Your stress-free life helps you maintain a youthful disposition, both physically and mentally. So, eat lots of chocolate!"

— Elaine Sherman, *Book of Divine Indulgences*

"Women have many moods;
chocolate satisfies them all."

— *Anonymous*

"Never underestimate the power of chocolate."

— *Anonymous*

"Truffles are the royalty of homemade candy."

— *Lorraine Bodger*

"Biochemically, love is just like eating large amounts of chocolate."

— John Milton, *The Devil's Advocate*

"Giving chocolate to others
is an intimate form of
communication, a sharing of
deep, dark secrets."

— Milton Zelman, *publisher of*
Chocolate News

"Chocolate in any language
spells love."

— *Anonymous*

"The greatest tragedies were written by the Greeks and Shakespeare…neither knew chocolate."

— *Sandra Boynton*

"Hell hath no fury like a woman who has sworn off fudge and chocolate."

— *Anonymous*

"The 12-step chocolate program:
Never be more than 12 steps
away from chocolate."

— *Terry Moore*

"Flowers wilt, jewelry tarnishes, and candles burn out…but chocolate doesn't hang around long enough to get old."

— *Sr. Cocoa Loca*

"If you get melted chocolate all
over your hands, you're eating it
too slowly."

— *Anonymous*

"When I die,' I said to my friend, 'I'm not going to be embalmed. I'm going to be dipped.' Milk chocolate or bittersweet was the immediate concern."

— *Adrianne Marcus*

"Chocolate symbolizes, as does
no other food, luxury, comfort,
sensuality, gratification, and love."

— *Karl Petzke*

"If in fact you are what you eat, I am a 114-pound bar of bittersweet chocolate."

— *Lora Brody*

"Chocolate. Here today.
Gone today."

— *Anonymous*

"May your life be filled, as mine
has been, with love and laughter;
and remember, when things
are rough all you need is...
Chocolate."

— Geraldine Solon, *Chocolicious*

"I owe it all to little chocolate donuts."

— *John Belushi*

"Chocolate is the first luxury. It has so many things wrapped up in it: Deliciousness in the moment, childhood memories, and that grin-inducing feeling of getting a reward for being good."

— *Mariska Hargitay*

"There's more to life than chocolate, but not right now."

— *Anonymous*

"You know, I live a monastic lifestyle. No, I do. I do live in extremes, basically. I go back and forth. Once every six months, I'll have a day where I eat more chocolate than has ever been consumed by a human being."

— *Jim Carrey*

"A little chocolate a day keeps the doctor at bay."

— *Marcia Carrington*

"If there is one flavor that can cause Americans to salivate at the mention of the name, it is chocolate."

— *Craig Claiborne*

"Your friendship is better than chocolate! Well, anyway, it's right up there."

— *Julie Sutton*

"What food do you crave?
Ask the question with enough
smoldering emphasis on the last
word, and the answer is bound to
be chocolate."

— *Diane Ackerman*

"Your face makes my soul want to
eat chocolate pudding."

— *Andy Milonakis*

"Friends are the chocolate chips
of life."

— *Anonymous*

"Life without chocolate is life lacking something important."

— *Maria Colman Morton and Frederic Morton*

"Cooking is one of life's joys. Chocolate is one of life's pleasures."

— *Sara Perry*

"Do not disturb, unless there is chocolate involved."

— *Anonymous*

"Other things are just food. But chocolate's chocolate."

— *Patrick Skene Catling*

"There is no chocolate anonymous because no one wants to quit."

— *Anonymous*

"Flowers speak the language of love for some, but for others, it's chocolate that fans the flames."

— *Rebecca J. Pate*

"Never, ever get between a girl and her chocolate."

— *Anonymous*

"We have never believed anyone should have to wait until the sun is high in the heavens to begin enjoying chocolate."

— *Mary Goodbody*

"Man cannot live on chocolate alone. But woman sure can."

— *Anonymous*

"It's not that chocolates are
a substitute for love. Love
is a substitute for chocolate.
Chocolate is, let's face it, far
more reliable than a man."

— *Miranda Ingram*

"For some there's therapy; for the rest of us there's chocolate."

— *Anonymous*

"Like the final act of a play or the crescendo of a symphony, we expect a good chocolate sweet to leave us speechless, craving for more."

— *Suzanne Ausnit*

"I fantasize about a world where I'm in charge, chocolate makes you skinny, and everything is always 75 percent off."

— *Anonymous*

"For those who deny that when the taste buds are seeking excitement, drama and sweet satisfaction, it is neither the potato nor the cranberry to which we turn. It is chocolate."

—*Lorna J. Sass*

"Always keep a smile on your face, a rainbow in your heart, and some dark chocolate on hand."

— *Anonymous*

"I never met a chocolate
I didn't like."

— Deanna Troi, *Star Trek:
The Next Generation*

"My soul's had enough chicken soup. I want chocolate."

— *Anonymous*

"Truly wonderful masterpieces can be created with great skill and all will be acclaimed with great enthusiasm, simply because they are made with chocolate."

— *Jennie Reekie*

"Chocolate is the key to happiness."

— *Anonymous*

"You know how I like to describe the way chocolate makes people feel? Watch a child devour a candy bar — that's contentment."

— Sandra Ramage, Twentieth-Century American Chocolate Lover

"After the morning's cup of lilac chocolate, I would hurry back to my quarters. In Paris I was never hungry."

— *Colette*

"Forget love; I'd rather fall in chocolate."

— Unknown or attributed to Sandra J. Dykes, comedian

"Chocolate is the answer. Who cares what the question is."

— *Anonymous*

"Love is like swallowing hot chocolate before it has cooled off. It takes you by surprise at first, but keeps you warm for a long time."

— *Henri Frederic Amiel*

"Money can't buy happiness. But it can buy chocolate, which is kind of the same thing."

— *Anonymous*

"Chocolate is a perfect food, as wholesome as it is delicious, a beneficent restorer of exhausted power. It is the best friend of those engaged in literary pursuits."

— *Baron Justus von Liebig*

"Chocolate is nature's way of making up for Mondays."

— *Anonymous*

"Chocolate is heavenly, mellow, sensual, deep, dark, sumptuous, gratifying, potent, dense, creamy, seductive, suggestive, rich, excessive, silky, smooth, luxurious, celestial. Chocolate is downfall, happiness, pleasure, love, ecstasy, fantasy...chocolate makes us wicked, guilty, sinful, healthy, chic, happy."

— *Elaine Sherman*

"Please save the planet. It's the only one with chocolate."

— *Anonymous*

"Don't wreck a sublime chocolate experience by feeling guilty. Chocolate isn't like premarital sex. It will not make you pregnant. And it always feels good."

— *Lora Brody*

"All you need in life is a friend
who has chocolate."

—— *Anonymous*

"Chocolate is a divine, celestial drink, the sweat of the stars, the vital seed, divine nectar, the drink of the gods, panacea and universal medicine."

— *Geronimo Piperni (quoted by Antonio Lavedán, Spanish army surgeon, 1796)*

"When I am sad I shall eat
chocolate and sing happy songs."

— *Anonymous*

"When you select the right kind of chocolate it is like giving your insides a hug. Everyone needs a chocolate hug."

— *Jean Kelsey*

"Seven days without chocolate
makes one weak."

— *Anonymous*

"My therapist told me the way
to achieve true inner peace is to
finish what I start. So far today,
I have finished two bags of
M&M's and a chocolate cake.
I feel better already."

— *Dave Barry*

"Coffee makes it possible to get out of bed. Chocolate makes it worthwhile."

— *Anonymous*

"Life is like a box of chocolates.
You never know what you're
gonna get."

— *Forrest Gump*

"Chocolate! Now that is a word
that conjures up describable
ecstasies. Truffles, bonbons,
peppermint patties, lollipops,
cakes, cookies, and more.
Breathes there a man, woman or
child who has not lusted after it,
devoured it, and moments later
dreamed of it still?"

— *Elaine Gonzalez*

"All I really need is love, but a little chocolate now and then doesn't hurt."

— Lucy Van Pelt (Charles Schulz, *Peanuts*)

"There's nothing better than a good friend, except a good friend with chocolate."

— *Linda Grayson*

"Milk chocolate is a dairy product."

— *Anonymous*

"Fruit only angers my need for chocolate."

— *Jason Love*

"Exercise is a 'dirty' word. Every time I hear it, I wash my mouth out with chocolate."

—— *Anonymous*

"I never do any television without chocolate. That's my motto and I live by it. Quite often I write the scripts and I make sure there are chocolate scenes. Actually I'm a bit of a chocolate tart and will eat anything. It's amazing I'm so slim."

—— *Dawn French*

"Ideas should be clear and
chocolate thick."

— *Spanish proverb*

"It has been shown as proof positive
that carefully prepared chocolate
is as healthful a food as it is
pleasant; that it is nourishing and
easily digested…that it is above all
helpful to people who must do a
great deal of mental work."

— *Anthelme Brillat-Savarin*

"There are two kinds of people in the world: those who love chocolate, and communists."

— *Leslie Moak Murray*

"Strength is the capacity to break
a chocolate bar in four pieces
with your bare hands — and then
just eating one piece."

— *Judith Viorst*

"Everyone has their price. Mine
is chocolate."

— *Anonymous*

"Healthy eating tip: Eat a chocolate bar before each meal. It'll take the edge off your appetite so you'll eat less."

— *Anonymous*

"The best part of Easter is eating your children's candy while they are sleeping and trying to convince them the next morning that the chocolate rabbit came with one ear."

— Anna Quindlen

"My desire for chocolate has seldom abated, even in times of great peril."

— *Marcel Desaulniers*

"Keep calm and eat chocolate."

— *Anonymous*

"I listened wide-eyed, stupid. Glowing by her voice in the dim light. If chocolate was a sound, it would've been Constantine's voice singing. If singing was a color, it would've been the color of that chocolate."

— Kathryn Stockett, *The Help*

"Don't wreck a sublime chocolate experience by feeling guilty."

— *Lora Brody*

"Topped with clouds of marshmallows or whipped cream, a steaming cup of hot chocolate is the perfect start for any day. And at night before bed, there's nothing better for sweet dreams."

— *Sara Perry*

"I am not overweight. I am chocolate enriched."

— *Anonymous*

"As with most fine things, chocolate has its season. There is a simple memory aid that you can use to determine whether it is the correct time to order chocolate dishes: any month whose name contains the letter A, E, or U is the proper time for chocolate."

— Sandra Boynton, *Chocolate: The Consuming Passion*

"When no one understands me, chocolate is there."

— *Anonymous*

"I adore anything that contains chocolate, is covered by chocolate or has ever been in the same kitchen with chocolate."

— *Miss Piggy*

"I was like a chocolate in a box, looking well behaved and perfect in place, all the while harboring a secret center."

— Deb Caletti, *Honey, Baby, Sweetheart*

"Chocolate cake may not fix everything, but it's a darn good substitute."

— *Anonymous*

"It was like having a box of chocolates shut in the bedroom drawer. Until the box was empty it occupied the mind too much."

— Graham Greene, *The Heart of the Matter*

"When we don't have the words, chocolate can speak volumes."

— *Joan Bauer*

"I don't drown my sorrows; I suffocate them with chocolate."

— *Jerry Smith*

"There are four basic food groups: milk chocolate, dark chocolate, white chocolate and chocolate truffles."

— *Anonymous*

"Nothing is more romantic than chocolate."

— *Ted Allen*

"Chocolate makes the world
go round."

— *Anonymous*

"Venice is like eating an entire box of chocolate liqueurs in one go."

— *Truman Capote*

"Anything is good if it's made of chocolate."

— *Jo Brand*

"*Chocolate: The Consuming Passion* was written for the Chocolate Elite, the select millions who like chocolate in all its infinite variety, using 'like' as in 'I like to breathe.'"

— *Sandra Boynton*

"Life is short. Eat chocolate."

— *Anonymous*

"Once you consume chocolate, chocolate will consume you."

— *Anonymous*

"Chocolate, of course, is the stuff
of which fantasies are made.
Rich, dark, velvety-smooth
fantasies that envelop the senses
and stir the passions. Chocolate
is madness; chocolate is delight."

— *Judith Olney*

"If at first you don't succeed, have a chocolate."

— *Anonymous*

"Chocolate makes everyone smile
— even bankers."

— *Bonneville Strohecker,*
chocolatier

"Stressed is Desserts spelled backward."

— *Anonymous*

"I have this theory that chocolate slows down the aging process. It may not be true, but do I dare take the chance?"

— *Anonymous*

"Put 'Eat chocolate' at the top of your list of things to do today. That way, at least you'll get one thing done."

— *Anonymous*

"Chocolate is not an addiction; it is simply a real necessity."

— *Anonymous*

"Chocolate makes otherwise normal people melt into strange states of ecstasy."

— *John West*

"My heart belongs to chocolate."

— *Anonymous*

"Once in a while I say, 'Go for it,' and I eat chocolate."

— *Claudia Schiffer*

"If I must die, let it be death by chocolate."

— *Anonymous*

"What you see before you, my friend, is the result of a lifetime of chocolate."

— *Katharine Hepburn*

"If it ain't chocolate, it ain't breakfast."

— *Anonymous*

"Chocolate candies are the best. Sweet and dark, they melt on our tongues and linger in our mouths with a delicious creaminess that is part taste, part memory."

— *Mary Goodbody*

"Flowers and champagne may set the stage, but it's chocolate that steals the show."

— *Anonymous*

"Does the notion of chocolate preclude the concept of free will?"

— *Sandra Boynton*

"The divine drink, which builds up resistance and fights fatigue. A cup of this precious drink (cocoa) permits a man to walk for a whole day without food."

— *Montezuma, Aztec Emperor (c. 1480-1520)*

"Did you ever notice there are no recipes for leftover chocolate?"

— *Anonymous*

"Did you hear about the guy who found a bottle on the ocean? He opened it and out popped a genie. The genie gave him three wishes. The guy wished for $1 million, and poof, there was $1 million. Then he wished for a convertible, and poof, there was a convertible. Finally after scratching his head a bit, he wished he could be irresistible to all women: Poof! He turned into a box of chocolates."

— *Anonymous*

"I got to thinking about relationships and partial lobotomies. Two seemingly different ideas that might just be perfect together — like chocolate and peanut butter."

— *Sarah Jessica Parker*

"Chocolate is always a good idea."

— *Anonymous*

"I can recommend switching to chocolate for all you addictive types…Think of the advantages… Chocolate doesn't make you stupid and clumsy. It doesn't render you incapable of operating heaving machinery…You don't have to smuggle chocolate across the border…Possession, even possession with intent to sell is perfectly legal…and second-hand chocolate doesn't offend the people around you."

— *Linda Henley*

"I'd give up chocolate, but I'm not a quitter."

— *Anonymous*